World Cities

LONDON

Christine Hatt

*Special photography
by Chris Fairclough*

Belitha Press

First published in the UK in 2000 by

 Belitha Press Limited
London House, Great Eastern Wharf,
Parkgate Road, London SW11 4NQ

ISBN 1 84138 090 1 hardback
     1 84138 332 5 paperback

British Library Cataloguing in Publication Data
for this book is available from the British Library.

Printed in Hong Kong

Editor Stephanie Bellwood
Designer Helen James
Photographer Chris Fairclough
Map illustrator Lorraine Harrison
Picture researcher Kathy Lockley
Consultant Adrian Green, The Museum of London
Educational consultant Elizabeth Bassant

Additional images
Bridgeman Art Library London & New York /British Library,
London 8r, /Guildhall Library, Corporation of London 10b, 24b,
/Private Collection 9b, 9t, 40t, /Private Collection /Stapleton
Collection 41t, /Victoria and Albert Museum, London 40b;
Colorsport 35b; Robert Harding Picture Library 4, 31t, 36t,
39t; Hayes Davidson/Nick Wood 42t; Hulton Getty 11t, 27br:
© Museum of London 8l; Rex Features 11b, 35t, 38t, 38b, 39b,
41b; © Tate Gallery, London 1999 37b; © V & A Picture Library
42b; Weidenfeld Archives 10t, 26-27t, /Lloyds of London 24t.

Words in **bold** are explained in the glossary on pages 46 and 47.

CONTENTS

INTRODUCTION

London is the capital of the United Kingdom (UK), which is made up of Great Britain (England, Scotland and Wales) and Northern Ireland. The city lies in the south-east of England and covers an area of about 1,578 square kilometres on either side of the River Thames. With a population of over seven million, London is by far the largest city in the UK. Birmingham, the second largest, has just over one million inhabitants.

▲ This view of London shows two of the city's most famous landmarks – Tower Bridge, spanning the River Thames, and St Paul's Cathedral, with its large dome.

Financial centre

The oldest part of London is **the City**. This small area on the north bank of the Thames is often called the **Square Mile**. The City contains the Stock Exchange, the Bank of England and many other organizations that make it one of the most important financial centres in the world.

Cultural life

London is a world-class cultural centre. It has more than 40 theatres (see page 34), where audiences enjoy everything from musicals to William Shakespeare's plays. The city also contains many cinemas, concert halls, museums and art galleries (see pages 35-37).

Royal residence

English (later British) kings and queens have lived in London for almost 1,000 years. There are several royal palaces in the capital. St James's Palace was built by King Henry VIII in the 16th century. Since 1837 the monarch has lived in Buckingham Palace (see page 15).

LONDON

STATUS
Capital of the United Kingdom
of Great Britain and Northern Ireland

AREA
1,578 square kilometres

POPULATION
7,122,200 (1997)

GOVERNING BODY
32 local councils and the Corporation of London,
plus the 25-member Greater London Assembly

CLIMATE
Temperature averages 5°C in January
and 18°C in July

TIME ZONE
Greenwich Mean Time (Nov to end March)
British Summer Time (end March to end Oct)

CURRENCY
Sterling: 100 pence = 1 pound

OFFICIAL LANGUAGE
English

Nelson's Column ➤ towers over Trafalgar Square. It is 56 metres tall and the statue on top is of the naval hero Admiral Nelson (see page 15).

Local and national government

London is divided into 32 boroughs and the City. Each borough is run by a council and the City is run by the Corporation of London, led by the Lord Mayor. In 2000 Londoners elected a new Greater London Assembly to run the whole city (see page 42).

The national government of the UK is also based in London. It is made up of the **House of Commons** and the **House of Lords.** They meet in different chambers of the Palace of Westminster, a building usually known as the Houses of Parliament.

◄ The Houses of Parliament on the north bank of the Thames. The clock tower is known as Big Ben, but this is really the name of the huge bell inside.

MAPS OF THE CITY

These maps show you London as it is today. The area map shows the boundaries of London's 13 inner boroughs and **the City**. The street map gives a close-up view of central London. Many of the places mentioned in the book are marked.

THE INNER BOROUGHS

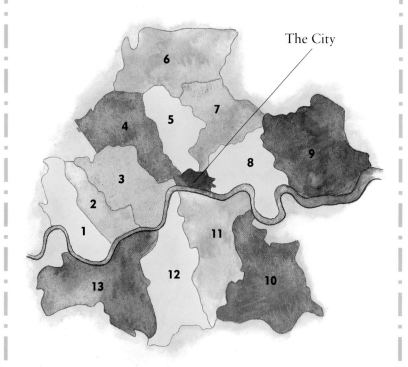

The City

Greater London (the whole London area) is divided into two parts: Inner London and Outer London. Inner London, shown above, contains 13 boroughs and the City. Outer London contains 19 boroughs.

1   Hammersmith and Fulham
2   Kensington and Chelsea
3   Westminster
4   Camden
5   Islington
6   Haringey
7   Hackney
8   Tower Hamlets
9   Newham
10 Lewisham
11 Southwark
12 Lambeth
13 Wandsworth

CENTRAL LONDON

REGENT'S CANAL

THE SERPENTINE

1	Natural History Museum	14	Eros, Piccadilly Circus	27	Royal National Theatre
2	Science Museum	15	National Gallery	28	Dr Johnson's House
3	Victoria and Albert Museum	16	Trafalgar Square	29	Old Bailey
4	Royal Albert Hall	17	Nelson's Column	30	St Paul's Cathedral
5	Albert Memorial	18	The Cenotaph	31	Museum of London
6	Hyde Park	19	St James's Palace	32	Barbican Centre
7	Central London Mosque	20	St James's Park	33	Bank of England
8	Regent's Park	21	Buckingham Palace	34	The City (see boroughs map)
9	Madame Tussaud's	22	Westminster Cathedral	35	Lloyd's of London
10	British Museum	23	Westminster Abbey	36	Globe Theatre
11	Shaftesbury Avenue	24	Tate Gallery	37	London Bridge
12	Covent Garden	25	Houses of Parliament	38	Tower of London
13	Soho	26	Westminster Bridge	39	Tower Bridge

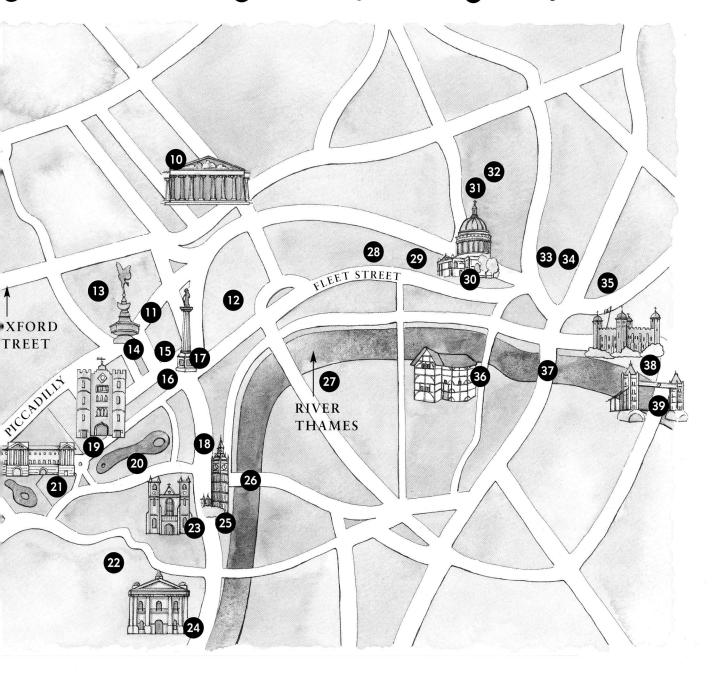

The Romans invaded England in 43 AD. They landed in Kent, made their way to the River Thames and sailed up it. Then they settled in a place on the north bank, where the river was not too wide. This settlement was called Londinium. A bridge was later built across the Thames.

◄ Oil lamps were used for lighting in Roman London. This foot-shaped lamp was made in Holland and brought to the city by ship.

Roman London

Tribes in England fought the Romans. The Iceni tribe, led by Queen Boudicca, burned down Londinium in 61 AD. The Romans later defeated the tribes and restored Londinium. It became the capital of Roman Britain. A **basilica, forum** and fort were built, plus a wall around the city. The Romans ruled until 410.

Saxons and Vikings

Later in the 5th century, **Saxons** settled just west of Londinium and formed the town of Lundenwic. It was raided by Danish **Vikings** in the 9th century. **Alfred the Great** defeated the Vikings in 886 and rebuilt the Roman city. In 1016 the Vikings triumphed again and ruled until 1042, when Edward the Confessor took over.

Medieval London

After Edward came King Harold in 1066. Later that year he was defeated by William, a **Norman** duke. William I (the Conqueror) was crowned king in Westminster Abbey (see page 22). In the following years London grew rapidly, and by 1300 about 80,000 people lived there. The **Black Death** of 1348-50 killed about half this population.

▲ This picture from around 1500 shows the Tower of London, which was at that time a prison.

Tudor London

London grew in importance under **Tudor** rule. King Henry VIII created palaces such as St James's. He is also famous for closing the country's monasteries in 1536, after the Catholic Church refused to grant him a divorce. During the reign of Elizabeth I, London was a wealthy and successful city. Theatre became popular, helped by the arrival of playwright William Shakespeare some time between 1585 and 1593.

▲ Each November people remember the Gunpowder Plot by burning dummies of Guy Fawkes (third from right) who planted the explosives.

Stuart London

The first **Stuart** king, James I, came to the throne in 1603. In 1605 a group of men tried to blow up both him and the Houses of Parliament. This **Gunpowder Plot** failed. In 1625 Charles I came to the throne. **Civil war** broke out in 1642 between supporters of the king and parliamentary forces, led by a **Puritan** called Oliver Cromwell. Charles I was beheaded in 1649 and Britain became a republic known as **the Commonwealth**. In 1660 the monarchy returned.

Plague and fire

London suffered two disasters in later Stuart years. In 1665 the Great Plague killed about 70,000 people. In 1666 the Great Fire destroyed almost all of **the City** and a large area to the west. Thousands of new houses were built, and Christopher Wren constructed St Paul's Cathedral (see page 15) as well as many churches.

◄ The Great Fire of London broke out in a bakery on 2 September, 1666, and burned strongly for almost four days. It left over 100,000 people homeless.

In 1714 George I came to the throne and the **Georgian** era began. London quickly grew in size and in 1801 the population reached about one million. Merchants and bankers grew rich, and many lived in the new **West End**. Other people suffered terrible poverty. Thousands lived in filthy **East End** slums, where disease, crime and drunkenness were common.

▲ Hanover Square was constructed in the early 18th century. It is typical of the many large, elegant squares built in this era.

Victorian London

Queen Victoria came to the throne in 1837. During her reign, Britain became a mighty industrial power, the **British Empire** grew, and there was a building boom in the capital. The railway arrived, **suburbs** developed and the population soared. When Victoria died in 1901, over six million people lived in London.

The First World War

The **First World War** began in 1914. The first air raid hit London in 1915, and during the war over 835 people were killed in air attacks. While the men were away, women did their jobs. Before the war, **suffragettes** had been campaigning for votes for women. In 1918, the year the war ended, women over 30 were allowed to vote for the first time.

In 1851 an event called ➤ the Great Exhibition of the Works of Industry of all Nations was held in London. It took place in a huge glass building called Crystal Palace.

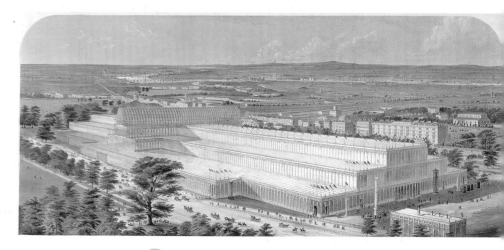

The Second World War

In 1939 the **Second World War** broke out and 690,000 children were moved out of London. Unfortunately many of them had returned when **the Blitz** began in 1940. The German bombing went on until May 1941. In 1944 flying bombs and rockets began to fall on the city. By the end of the war 30,000 people had been killed in London and many of the city's buildings lay in ruins.

▲ Londoners tried to live as normally as possible during the Blitz. Here a postman delivers letters among the ruins of a street.

▲ Protesters and police at the 1990 Poll Tax riot. The Poll Tax was replaced with a different type of tax in 1993.

A new era

London slowly recovered from the war. In 1951 the Festival of Britain was held on the south bank of the River Thames. Two years later, Queen Elizabeth II was crowned in Westminster Abbey. In the 1960s, the capital became 'Swinging London'. Young people in the city shopped in Carnaby Street boutiques and danced to new bands such as the Beatles.

The millennium and beyond

Unemployment grew in London in the 1960s and '70s, as docks closed and traditional industries declined (see pages 24-25). In the 1980s, banking, insurance and tourism boomed, and Docklands redevelopment began (see page 19). An anti-**Poll Tax** riot and **IRA** bombs rocked the city in the 1990s. Londoners began the third millennium by electing a new citywide government and mayor (see page 42).

THE PEOPLE OF LONDON

London is a growing city with a population of more than seven million. It is also a multicultural city, as it has been since Roman times. Now about a quarter of the capital's inhabitants are members of **ethnic minorities**.

The Irish community

The largest non-English group in London is the Irish community. People from Ireland first went to London in large numbers in 1845, when disease killed their potato crops, leading to famine. Many still emigrate there. The city's Irish-born population is over 250,000, and there are also many people who were born in London but have Irish parents.

▲ A street in Southall, in west London. Punjabi immigrants there have opened Indian food and clothes shops. Their London-born children often combine Indian and British lifestyles.

Indian communities

Indians are London's largest ethnic minority, with a population of about 411,000. Many came to the city after India became independent from Britain in 1947. Thousands more arrived from Uganda and Kenya in the 1960s, when these countries forced them to leave. Most settled in Outer London boroughs. Many Punjabi Sikhs, for example, live in Hounslow.

▲ In and around Brick Lane, street signs are written in English and also in Bengali, the language of Bangladesh.

Pakistanis and Bangladeshis

Thousands of Pakistanis and Bangladeshis live in London, mostly in the east. The Inner London borough of Tower Hamlets is home to about half the city's Bangladeshis. The heart of the community is a street called Brick Lane, lined with inexpensive restaurants that attract Londoners and tourists alike.

Caribbeans and Africans

Black Caribbeans are London's second largest ethnic minority. They come from islands such as Jamaica and from Guyana. Caribbeans first arrived in large numbers after the **Second World War**. Most now live in Inner London boroughs such as Lambeth. Black Africans from countries such as Nigeria are London's third largest ethnic minority.

Racism and riots

London's minorities have often suffered racism. In 1958 there were riots against Caribbeans in Notting Hill. In the 1970s skinheads attacked Bangladeshis in Brick Lane. Many black people rioted against discrimination in Brixton and Tottenham in the 1980s. The racial situation in London is slowly improving, but there are still problems (see page 26).

A street market in Brixton, a south London ▼ area with a large Afro-Caribbean population. African and Caribbean foods are sold here.

RELIGIOUS REFUGEES

In the past the **East End** was a refuge for two groups of people escaping religious persecution. **Huguenots** from France arrived in the 17th century after their Protestant religion was banned. In the late 19th century Jews fleeing **pogroms** in Russia and Central Europe came to London. Many Jews live in North London. Some belong to ultra-**orthodox** groups (below).

A young population

London's population has been rising since the mid-1980s. **Asylum-seekers** from abroad have contributed to this increase. Other new inhabitants are single young people attracted by jobs or universities. Retired people and couples with children often leave the capital. This means that London's population is younger than the UK's as a whole.

BUILDINGS AND BRIDGES

London lost many buildings in the Great Fire and **the Blitz** (see pages 9 and 11). But the city still contains magnificent architecture from the past as well as some dazzling new structures.

▲ Tower Bridge, completed in 1894. Machinery in its two huge towers raises the roadway to let tall ships pass underneath.

London's bridges

Thirty-five bridges span the Thames in Greater London. The oldest is London Bridge, which was originally made of wood. In 1209 it was replaced by a stone bridge with shops and houses along its sides. This was followed by a granite bridge in 1831, and the present concrete bridge in 1973.

The Tower of London

The Tower of London contains 20 towers. The White Tower at its centre, built by William the Conqueror (see page 8), is the oldest. The Tower of London is home to the Crown Jewels, and is where two of Henry VIII's wives were beheaded.

Westminster's palaces

The Palace of Westminster was built by Edward the Confessor (see page 8) and rebuilt by William the Conqueror. William's son added Westminster Hall. The palace burned down in 1834, but was later rebuilt and is now known as the Houses of Parliament. Inside is Westminster Hall, which survived the fire.

t Paul's Cathedral

t Paul's Cathedral was built between 1675
nd 1711 by Sir Christopher Wren (see page 40).
: replaced Old St Paul's, lost in the Great Fire.
Vren's church has a distinctive dome. At the
ome's base is the Whispering Gallery. A whisper
> the wall on one side can be heard on the other.

MONUMENTS

London is packed with
monuments. Nelson's Column
in Trafalgar Square shows
Admiral Nelson, who
defeated the French at the
Battle of Trafalgar in 1805.
The statue of Eros (right) in
Piccadilly Circus is a memorial
to the Earl of Shaftesbury,
who improved 19th-
century working
conditions for the poor.
The Albert Memorial is a
tribute to Queen Victoria's
husband, Prince Albert.

▲ The East Front of Buckingham Palace.
When the queen is at the palace,
a flag flies on top of the building.

Buckingham Palace

Buckingham Palace is the London home of the British
oyal family. It was completed in 1705 for the Duke of
Buckingham, but later sold to George III. Queen Victoria
made it her official residence in 1837. Eighteen of the
palace's 600 rooms open to the public during the summer.

Canary Wharf Tower

The tallest building in the UK is in Canary Wharf, part
f London's Docklands (see page 11). One Canada
quare, known as Canary Wharf Tower, is 244 metres
igh and covered in glinting stainless steel. A white
ght flashes on the top to warn aircraft that it is there.

▲ Canary Wharf Tower opened in
1991. It is full of offices, and some
of Britain's biggest newspaper
companies are based there.

OPEN SPACES

Green open spaces, from formal parks to rough, open land, cover about a tenth of Greater London. Many are on the outskirts of the capital, but even the crowded **West End** and **City** have plenty of attractive parks and gardens.

Central London parks

Hyde Park covers 140 **hectares**. It is next to the 111-hectare Kensington Gardens, and together they form the largest green space in the centre of the city. Hyde Park contains the Serpentine boating lake and Speaker's Corner, where anyone can make a speech. Regent's Park, to the north, has houses designed by John Nash (see page 18), plus London Zoo and an open-air theatre.

▲ Hyde Park is a peaceful place to relax. It is also the venue for many big open-air events such as concerts and protest marches.

▲ Fortunately, British monarchs did not hunt down all the deer in Richmond Park. Many descendants of ancient herds live there today.

Richmond and Hampton Court

Two former royal palaces in West London Richmond and Hampton Court, are surrounded by beautiful parks. Richmond Park covers over 800 hectares, making it one of the largest in Europe. It was once a hunting ground for kings such as Henry VIII, and deer still roam there. Hampton Court Gardens cover about 270 hectares and include formal flower beds, wide avenues of trees and a maze.

The Royal Botanic Gardens

The Royal Botanic Gardens in Kew contain the world's largest plant collection, built up from the 18th century by botanists Joseph Banks and William Hooker. In the gardens are 30,000 types of living plants, as well as dried plants and seeds. Buildings include the Palm House greenhouse, the Princess of Wales Conservatory and a tower called a pagoda.

Hampstead Heath

Hampstead Heath in North London is the capital's largest area of rough, open land. Its landmarks include Parliament Hill, where people go to fly kites, and Boudicca's Mound, the legendary burial site of Queen Boudicca (see page 8). The 18th-century Kenwood House is also here. It contains many famous paintings, and summer concerts are held in its grounds.

▲ The Palm House at Kew was completed in 1848 and contained palm trees. Now it is home to all sorts of tropical trees and flowers.

▲ The pagoda in Battersea Park was given to London in 1985 by an order of Buddhist monks and nuns.

Public parks

Until the mid-19th century, all London's main parks were on royal land in the rich parts of the city. Then the government decided that new, public parks should be created in poor areas. The first, Victoria Park in Hackney, opened in 1845. It was followed by many others, including Battersea Park in 1858. Battersea contains a children's zoo and peace pagoda, and has an Easter Parade every year.

RIVER LIFE

The River Thames runs through London for about 50 km. By the mid-20th century, the river was polluted with industrial waste and sewage. The London section contained no fish at all. Since then, a clean-up campaign has brought back 115 species of fish, as well as birds such as herons. In 1996 the Thames Path opened to allow people to walk along most of the river from the Thames Barrier in the east to Hampton Court in the west and beyond.

HOMES AND HOUSING

Before the Great Fire, most Londoners had wooden homes in **the City** (see page 19). After the Fire, London expanded and building styles were more varied. People now live in all kinds of houses and flats.

▲ Georgian architect John Nash built terraces of elegant mansions, including Cumberland Terrace (above), on the edge of Regent's Park.

Georgian growth

London expanded fast in the **Georgian** era and its slum areas grew. At the same time, spacious new homes were built in **West End** areas such as Mayfair. These were often arranged in terraces and squares, which became very fashionable. Many of these graceful homes still stand. Now, as then, only rich people can afford to live in them.

Victorian terraces

In Victorian times the new railways (see page 28) made it possible for people to work in the centre of London but live on the outskirts. As a result, **suburbs** of affordable, red-brick terraced houses were built. These are still homes for Londoners, but many are now divided into flats.

▲ George Peabody was an American ex-banker who built homes for poor Londoners in the 19th century. This is one of his works, Peabody Square.

Home improvement

The Victorians also improved housing conditions for London's poor. At first, charities or individuals built homes for the needy. Then, in 1890, the Housing of the Working Classes Act was passed and local governments began to clear slums and build council housing. This was affordable for poorer people.

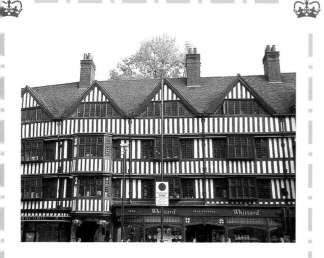

HISTORIC HOUSES

After the Great Fire of London in 1666, people were no longer allowed to build wooden houses – they had to use brick instead. A few timber-framed houses remain from pre-Fire days, including Staple Inn, Holborn (above), now used as offices. Another survivor is 17 Fleet Street. Inside is Prince Henry's Room, which contains original oak panels and stained glass. Some of the possessions of Samuel Pepys are kept here. He was a Londoner who wrote a famous diary covering many important events in the 1660s, such as the Great Fire.

Post-war housing

During the **Second World War** 130,000 homes in London were destroyed. The housing crisis was solved by moving people to **New Towns** and building council estates. The estates were often made up of poor-quality concrete tower blocks. After a block called Ronan Point collapsed in 1968, low-rise housing was built and many high-rise homes were demolished.

Thousands of people ➤ work in the City, but hardly any live there. The Barbican housing development was completed in 1982 to try to attract more people to the area.

Spreading suburbs

In the 1920s and '30s London's transport networks grew and over a million people moved out to newly connected suburbs. The suburbs with Underground links were known as Metroland, and many semi-detached houses were built there. These homes are still popular. More council homes were also built outside central London in this era.

Housing today

London now contains over three million homes. Most are owned rather than rented, as council tenants have had the right to buy their flats and houses since 1980. Developers are now building more private homes, especially in fashionable areas such as Docklands. Housing associations work to provide more homes for the poor. But thousands of Londoners still live in temporary accommodation and hundreds sleep on the streets.

EDUCATION

Until the late 19th century, London schools were run by churches and charities. Many children received no education. In 1880 a new law ordered children to attend school up to the age of eleven. Now all British children must go to school between the ages of five and sixteen.

▲ Hundreds of red-brick primary schools like this were built in London after 1880. Many are now in urgent need of modernization.

Starting early

Although the official school starting age is five, the British government encourages parents to send their young children to nurseries. Over half of London's three- and four-year-olds go to school. Often they attend for just a few days a week, or for half days only. Primary education, for all children, is usually at an infants' school from ages five to seven, then at a junior school until eleven.

Secondary system

Secondary-age pupils must attend school until they are sixteen, but can stay on to eighteen. Until the 1950s, they went to schools called secondary moderns, or to more academic grammar schools. Then comprehensives, where all pupils are taught together, were built. London's first was Kidbrooke School, Woolwich (1954).

Private schools

Some secondary-level pupils go to private, fee-paying schools. Four in London are particularly famous. Westminster School, near Westminster Abbey, has existed since the 12th century. St Paul's School was founded near the old cathedral in 1509, but is now in Barnes, in the south-west. Harrow, in the north-west, opened in 1572. Dulwich College, in the south, dates from 1619.

The large, looming structure of Senate House in central London contains the main library and administrative buildings of London University.

London's universities

There are thirteen universities in London. The city's first university, University College, was set up in 1826 for non-**Anglicans**, who were barred from Oxford and Cambridge universities. It joined King's College to form the University of London, which now has many more colleges.

Careers training

School-leavers may choose to train for a career rather than go to university. Some join the Youth Training scheme, take a government-sponsored job and learn a trade. They work towards National Vocational Qualifications (NVQs).

◄ Pupils of the exclusive and expensive Harrow School have included former prime ministers Robert Peel and Winston Churchill. Peel also founded the Metropolitan Police.

THE ROYAL SOCIETY

Although London had no university until the 19th century, it did have specialist schools of art and medicine, as well as many learned societies. The greatest of these was the Royal Society, which was set up in Oxford but moved to London in 1659. The society's aim was to discuss and publish scientific ideas. It still exists and is based in the grand Carlton House Terrace (below), near Buckingham Palace. Christopher Wren (see page 40) was its president from 1680 to 1681.

Many Londoners still call themselves Christians, but now members of other religions, such as Islam, also live in the capital.

The Church of England

King Henry VIII set up the Church of England in 1534. It is still the country's official church and has many London members. The city has three great **Anglican** churches – St Paul's Cathedral (see page 15), Southwark Cathedral and Westminster Abbey, where Britain's kings and queens are crowned. Poets' Corner in the abbey contains the tombs of many famous writers, including Charles Dickens (see page 40).

▲ Edward the Confessor (see page 8) built Westminster Abbey, which was a monastery until Henry VIII's reign. Its towers were added in the 1700s.

Roman Catholicism

Henry VIII's split from the Roman Catholic church (see page 9) led to centuries of anti-Catholic feeling. Then, in the 19th century, many Irish Catholics arrived in London and the post of Archbishop of Westminster was created. In 1903 a new Catholic church, Westminster Cathedral, opened.

Westminster Cathedral is an ➤ elaborate and unusual striped building. Inside it contains several colourful chapels. A lift takes visitors to the top of the beautifully decorated main tower.

Islam

Many members of London's large Islamic community are Bangladeshis and Pakistanis (see page 12). Others, such as Arabs and Turks, belong to smaller minority groups. The city's Islamic places of worship, called mosques, range from ordinary local buildings to the impressive Central London Mosque in Regent's Park.

GOOD WORKS

Over the years, Christians in London have founded many organizations to help people in trouble. William Booth set up the Salvation Army in 1865 to convert people to Christianity and give them practical help. It still runs hostels for the homeless. In 1953 the Reverend Chad Varah founded the Samaritans in the church of St Stephen Walbrook. Since then, anyone with a problem has been able to phone a member of the organization at any time of the day or night.

▲ This building on Brick Lane (see page 12) was built as a **Huguenot** church. It was later a synagogue and finally became a mosque.

▼ The ornate Asian-style beauty of the Swaminarayan Temple makes it stand out sharply from the ordinary London streets around.

Judaism

London's Jewish community grew in the 19th century, when refugees came from Russia (see page 13), and again in the 20th century, when Jews came from **Nazi** Germany. Many of the city's 196,000 Jews live in northern areas such as Golders Green and worship in synagogues there. London's oldest synagogue, Bevis Marks (1701), is in a different area, **the City**.

Hinduism

Many of the Indians living in London are Hindus. In 1995 some built a magnificent place of worship in the north-western suburb of Neasden. It is called the Swaminarayan Temple, and all its many parts were carved from marble and limestone in India, then sent to London to be assembled.

INDUSTRY AND FINANCE

From Roman times until the late 20th century, London had a large port, but it slowly lost importance. Traditional industries such as clothes-making have also declined. But new industries such as tourism are growing and **the City** remains a leading financial centre.

 Many cargoes, such as sugar, spices and coffee, were brought to London's bustling port. Here men are unloading Indian tea.

The Port of London

In the Middle Ages, London's port made the city a major centre for the export of wool and the import of wine. In the 19th century, thousands of ships brought goods to London from all over the **British Empire**. The port grew until the 1960s, when the Empire broke up. The docks then became out of date and ships went elsewhere. Between 1967 and 1981 all the docks closed and about 25,000 people lost their jobs.

TRADE GUILDS

In the Middle Ages, different professions, for example goldsmiths or fishmongers, formed groups called guilds. Each guild looked after the business interests of its members and had a meeting hall. The hall on the right still belongs to the Mercers, who were cloth dealers. Guilds are now called livery companies, and most are social rather than professional organizations. New livery companies are still being created for new professions.

Industrial decline

As London grew in the early 20th century, so did its industry. Many people began to work in new car and electrical goods factories. After the **Second World War**, cheap imports and better-quality goods such as Japanese electronics put many firms out of business. Others moved out to where rents and wage costs were lower.

New industries

London's traditional industries are still dying out. From 1986 to 1996, the capital's manufacturing jobs fell by over a third. But some new industries are booming. In 1996, 25.5 million tourists visited London, providing many people with work. There are also new jobs in Information Technology (IT). Even so, unemployment in London is above the national average.

▲ London's tourist trade provides jobs in hotels, restaurants and museums. Some people work as drivers or guides on open-topped tour buses.

The newspaper industry

Fleet Street was the centre of London's newspaper industry from 1702. England's oldest daily paper, *The Times*, was first printed nearby in 1788. By the 1980s, new computer technology was threatening the jobs of Fleet Street printers. They did not want to change, but most papers moved to new offices in Docklands and began to use modern working methods.

Making money

The City has been a financial centre since the 16th century. Its major buildings include the Bank of England, which is the government bank, and the Stock Exchange, where people buy and sell stocks and shares. Lloyd's of London, an important insurance organization, is also here. Almost a third of London's jobs are in finance and business, and the number is rising.

◄ The Lloyd's of London insurance business began in the 17th century. The organization moved into this striking building in 1986.

Over the centuries all kinds of crimes have been committed in London. Punishments have been varied. In the **Tudor** era, traitors had their heads stuck on poles at London Bridge. In **Georgian** times, many criminals were hanged, watched by huge crowds. The worst that modern law-breakers face is a prison sentence.

London's police

London's main police force, the Metropolitan Police, was founded by Robert Peel in 1829. The City of London Police, responsible for the **Square Mile**, was set up ten years later. The forces are separate, but wear similar navy blue uniforms. The Metropolitan Police headquarters is New Scotland Yard. Its officers' duties include protecting the queen.

Capital crime

London's most common crimes are theft, handling stolen goods and burglary. In 1996, these were ten times more frequent than violent attacks. Racial crime was highlighted in 1993 when teenager Stephen Lawrence was killed because he was black. An inquiry found that the Metropolitan Police had been racist in the way they dealt with the case. They are now trying to improve, for example by recruiting more black and Asian officers.

◄ London police officers are always ready to assist passers-by. They keep in touch with the local police station by radio.

Security services

Britain has two London-based security services, MI5 and MI6. In the past, MI5's main role was to prevent foreign spies from collecting secret information here, but in 1992, during an **IRA** bombing campaign in London, MI5 took on some anti-terrorist duties too. MI6 members often work abroad, but their London home is a huge new building on the south bank of the river.

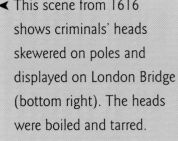

◀ This scene from 1616 shows criminals' heads skewered on poles and displayed on London Bridge (bottom right). The heads were boiled and tarred.

JACK THE RIPPER

Jack the Ripper is the nickname given to one of the most infamous criminals ever to stalk the streets of London. He brutally killed six women in the Whitechapel district of the **East End** in 1888 (below). Then the murders mysteriously stopped. The killer was never caught or identified, although many people were suspected. These included a member of the royal family, a famous painter, a surgeon and a barrister, Montague Druitt. Druitt was the most likely culprit.

This statue is on top ➤ of the Old Bailey and represents justice. The scales symbolize the careful weighing up of evidence in court.

Courts and chambers

The centre of legal London is just west of **the City**. The four **Inns of Court** are there, plus the Royal Courts of Justice. Most criminal cases are tried in the Central Criminal Court, known as the Old Bailey. This court lies in the City itself, where it was built on the site of the old Newgate Prison.

Until the early 19th century, Londoners got around by walking, taking boats along the river or riding in horse-drawn carriages. Then more bridges and roads were built, railways and cars arrived and the complex transport web of the modern capital developed.

Railway rides

The railways came to London in Victorian times. The first important station was Euston, which opened in 1837. Others quickly followed, including Paddington in 1838, later redesigned by the great engineer Isambard Kingdom Brunel. London now has seven major stations providing both long-distance and local services. Eurostar trains run from Waterloo Station to the **Channel Tunnel** and on into mainland Europe.

▲ Liverpool Street Station in **the City** is the busiest station in London. High roofs provide space for shops and restaurants.

Baker Street Station was on London's first ▼ Underground line. Two of its platforms have been restored to show how they used to look.

Going underground

London's Underground network, the world's first, opened in 1863. The 'tube' now has 12 lines and over 400 km of track. About 2.5 million passengers use it each day, but the tracks and signals are old and delays are common. Some improvements are being made, and an 11-station extension to the Jubilee Line opened in December 1999. It runs from west to east, providing a route from central London to Docklands (see page 43).

London's buses

London's double-decker red buses are famous. The city has nearly 1,000 bus routes and buses of many other types and colours also travel on them. Many double-deckers are now operated by one person and have closing doors instead of an open platform. Some have a platform that lowers so that wheelchair users can board easily.

▲ Old-style 'Routemaster' buses like this have a conductor who collects fares and issues tickets.

THE REGENT'S CANAL

Canals were an important means of transport in Britain during the **Industrial Revolution**. The Regent's Canal opened in 1820. It was part of a network carrying cargoes from London's port to the North of England and bringing coal and other goods back. The canal is nearly 14 km long and runs north of Regent's Park. Pleasure boats now travel along it, and houseboats are moored in parts of the canal such as Little Venice (below).

Capital cars

Driving in London is often an unpleasant experience. Traffic jams are frequent. Many occur on the M25 motorway around the city, which was built in 1986 to improve traffic flow. London's black taxis can usually find a way through the busy streets. Their drivers must pass a difficult test, called the Knowledge, before they are allowed to carry passengers.

Air travel

There are seven airports in the London area. The most important are Heathrow and Gatwick, which are both some distance from the centre. The city's air traffic is growing and a fifth Heathrow terminal is planned. Many people are opposed to this because of the pollution and noise more aeroplanes will create.

Docklands Light Railway

The Docklands Light Railway (DLR) is a system of automatic, driverless trains that run to the Docklands area. It opened in 1987 and in 1991 was linked to the Central Line of the Underground network.

SHOPS AND MARKETS

Most medieval Londoners did their shopping in **the City**, especially in the bustling Cheapside area. As the **West End** developed, the number of stalls and shops there grew. Now shops are found all over the capital and people come from far and wide to spend their money in London.

Oxford Street

Oxford Street is one of London's busiest shopping areas. Many of its smaller shops sell tourist souvenirs, but there are stylish department stores, too. The most famous is Selfridge's, opened in 1909 by an American, Gordon Selfridge. Oxford Street also has two Marks and Spencer stores. The first 'M and S' shops were penny bazaars, where all goods cost a penny. They grew into a huge food and clothing chain.

Knightsbridge

The Knightsbridge area of London is home to the biggest department store not only in the city but in the whole of Britain. This is Harrods, which has about 330 departments. Its domed, terracotta building is lit up spectacularly at night. Nearby is Harvey Nichols, which caters for the young rich. The latest clothes, make-up, perfumes and foods can all be found there.

▲ Crowds, traffic and aching feet are all part of the Oxford Street shopping experience. At Christmas people pack the pavements until it is hard to move.

Harrods was a small shop when it ➤ opened in 1849. Now it covers 1.6 **hectares**. About 11,500 bulbs are needed to light up the store at night.

ART AND ANTIQUES

The St James's and Mayfair districts are the centre of the fine art and antiques trade in London. The capital's two grandest auction houses, Sotheby's (below) and Christie's, are here. So, too, are some of the best private art galleries. Bond Street galleries usually specialize in old paintings. Cork Street galleries often show works by daring new artists.

Specialist shops

Many of London's specialist shops are clustered in the wealthy areas of St James's and Piccadilly. In Jermyn Street, shoppers can buy expensive top hats at Bates or perfumes at Floris. On Piccadilly, they can visit the grand Fortnum and Mason food hall. In the chic shops of Burlington Arcade, they can splash out on everything from cashmere to leather.

Food markets

London has many kinds of food market. Billingsgate Fish Market stood in the City for hundreds of years, but moved to Docklands in 1982. Smithfield Meat Market remains on its old City site, but farmers no longer bring cattle there to sell. The 600-year-old Leadenhall Market is now in a beautiful Victorian ironwork building in the City. It sells fine foods such as caviar, pheasants and Stilton cheese.

Crafts and clothes

In 1974 London's main fruit and vegetable market moved out of Covent Garden. The old market hall now contains shops and restaurants, as well as craft and clothes stalls. The weekend market at Camden Lock, on the Regent's Canal (see page 29), is another popular place to look for crafts, especially jewellery, as well as fashionable clothing.

▲ Covent Garden was originally the garden of a convent. Now it is a bustling area where tourists busily search for bargains.

FOOD AND DRINK

For many years, people in Britain were mocked for their unimaginative diet of meat, boiled vegetables and steamed puddings. There has now been a food and drink revolution in the country, and especially in London.

At home, Londoners are now as likely to eat curry as chops, and restaurants offer a huge variety of meals.

British cooking

British cooking is popular in many London eating places. These include Rules, which opened in 1798 and is the city's oldest restaurant – Charles Dickens was a regular customer. Diners enjoy its formal atmosphere and traditional meats and pies. Some restaurants serve 'modern British' cuisine, which is classic dishes with a twist, such as mashed potato with garlic.

▲ The light, spacious interior of Rules restaurant. The walls are decorated with paintings and old advertising posters for plays staged in London.

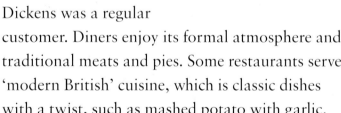

Everyday eating

Once, many Londoners had a fried bacon-and-egg breakfast. Now people often choose healthier food, such as cereal or toast. Sandwiches are a common lunchtime snack. Evening meals may be anything from pie and chips to a pasta or rice dish. For Sunday lunch, the old British favourite of roast meat and potatoes is still a popular choice.

Tea and coffee

Londoners are famous for their love of a good cup of tea, at home, at work and in cafés. Coffee has been drunk in London since the 17th century, when coffee houses were hotbeds of political discussion and debate. Nowadays American-style bars, selling fashionable coffees such as cappuccinos, are everywhere.

PUBLIC HOUSES

London is packed full of pubs (public houses), where people go to drink beer or wine, and perhaps order a bar meal. Some have fascinating histories. The Angel pub in Docklands dates back to the 15th century and once sold beer made by local monks. Ye Olde Cheshire Cheese on Fleet Street was founded in 1667. It is particularly famous for its excellent steak and kidney puddings.

This Chinese restaurant ▼ in Soho has a display of Peking duck in the window. To prepare this dish, the duck meat is coated with vinegar and honey, then left to dry before cooking.

Indian and Chinese food

Thanks to the capital's multicultural population, most Londoners have learned to enjoy cooking from other countries. Indian food is especially popular and many people often eat at their local 'curry house'. London also contains gourmet Indian restaurants such as Veeraswamy's, the oldest in the capital. Chinese food is a favourite, too. The streets of Soho's Chinatown are lined with restaurants offering such specialities as Peking duck.

Take-away food

London has thousands of burger and chicken fast-food restaurants. It also has many Indian, Chinese and pizza take-aways. These will often deliver food to people's homes. The city's fish and chip shops are part of a uniquely British take-away tradition. They sell deep-fried, battered fish, such as cod, and chunky chips flavoured with salt and vinegar.

▲ An Indian and an Italian restaurant stand side by side on a London street. The choice of food in the city is huge.

ENTERTAINMENT

 London is a great centre of all kinds of entertainment, and the streets of the city are busy by night as well as by day.

The Globe Theatre

One of London's first theatres was the Globe, completed in 1599. It stood on the south bank of the Thames and was where William Shakespeare (see page 9) worked. The theatre burned down, but in 1997 a copy opened close to the old site. Shakespeare's plays are now performed there in 16th-century style, without microphones or electric lights.

▲ The rebuilt Globe Theatre is a circular building made of timber and with a thatched roof, just like the original.

▲ Neon signs advertising top theatres such as the Lyric and the Apollo light up Shaftesbury Avenue at night.

Theatreland

In 1642 London's theatres were closed by Oliver Cromwell's **Puritans** (see page 9). They re-opened when the monarchy returned, and many new theatres were built. There are now 40 or more in the **West End**'s theatreland. London's most famous theatrical street, Shaftesbury Avenue, has six theatres which stage many popular plays and musicals.

Modern theatres

Two of London's most important theatres lie outside the West End. The National Theatre, now the Royal National, opened on the South Bank in 1976. Inside are three stages, where fine actors perform top-quality works. The Barbican Centre in **the City** opened in 1982. It has two theatres where the famous **Royal Shakespeare Company** stages plays.

THE BBC

The British Broadcasting Corporation (BBC) was founded in 1922. It runs two of Britain's main television channels, BBC1 and BBC2, and several new **digital** channels. It also has a radio network that includes five national stations and the international World Service. BBC managers work in Broadcasting House, in central London, and many programme-makers are based at Television Centre in West London.

Cinema culture

Most of the city's top cinemas, such as the Empire, are in Leicester Square. Glitzy film premières are often held there. A new IMAX cinema is now open on the South Bank. Developers are also planning to turn the Battersea Power Station into a leisure complex with a 35-screen cinema.

Stars of the film ➤ *Shakespeare in Love* attend its 1999 London première at the Empire in Leicester Square.

Sporting life

Wembley Stadium was London's major sports venue, used for football matches such as the **FA Cup** final. It closed in 2000, and is being replaced by a huge new stadium on the site. London's main rugby ground is Twickenham, while top-class cricket is played at Lord's and the Oval.

Music matters

London caters for music-lovers of all sorts. The city has five main orchestras and there are frequent classical music concerts at the Royal Festival Hall, Royal Albert Hall and Barbican Centre. Opera is staged at the Coliseum and at the newly modernized Royal Opera House in Covent Garden. The biggest pop music venues include Earl's Court and Wembley Arena.

England and Pakistan ➤ compete in a cricket match at the Oval in south London. The cricket ground opened in 1845. Before, the area was used for growing fruit and vegetables.

MUSEUMS AND ART GALLERIES

London has more than 300 museums and art galleries. Between them, they contain the most varied collection of treasures in the world.

▲ Amazing mummies from Ancient Egypt are always popular with visitors to the British Museum.

The British Museum

The British Museum is famous for its displays of Greek, Egyptian and other relics, including the **Rosetta Stone**. In 2000, a new and much praised Great Court was opened in its magnificent 19th-century building. The museum is London's most popular tourist attraction, receiving even more visitors than Madame Tussaud's waxworks.

South Kensington museums

Three museums stand side by side in South Kensington. The Victoria and Albert Museum (see page 42) specializes in treasures such as costumes and jewellery. The Natural History Museum is devoted to the natural world – the dinosaur display is especially popular. The Science Museum has everything from steam trains to space capsules. Children can try out experiments in its Launch Pad area.

The Museum of London

The Museum of London tells the capital's story from prehistoric times to the present. Exhibits include the golden Lord Mayor's Coach, which forms part of the procession at the Lord Mayor's Show each November.

The imposing Natural History Museum ▲ building was designed by architect Alfred Waterhouse. It opened in 1881.

Greenwich museums

The Greenwich area is home to the National Maritime Museum. The museum's displays cover many sea-related subjects, for example ships and the sea battles of British Admiral Horatio Nelson. The Old Royal Observatory, containing equipment for studying the stars, is nearby. The zero line of longitude runs through it and time around the world is measured from there.

◄ The *Cutty Sark* sailing ship once carried cargoes of tea from China to London. Now it is moored permanently at Greenwich and visitors can climb on board.

The National Gallery

There are about 2,200 paintings in the National Gallery on Trafalgar Square. The gallery's main wings contain paintings by Michelangelo, Rembrandt, Monet and other great artists from all over the world. The new Sainsbury wing, opened in 1991, contains the gallery's oldest works, by artists such as Leonardo da Vinci.

The Tate Gallery

Sir Henry Tate grew rich by inventing the sugar cube and used his money to found an art gallery on the north bank of the Thames. In 2000, its collection was divided. The old gallery, now Tate Britain, houses British art from 1500 to the present. Tate Modern, in a renovated power station on the south bank, houses modern international art.

DR JOHNSON

18th-century writer Dr Samuel Johnson compiled the first great English dictionary in London. He loved the city and once made this famous statement:

'...you find no man, at all intellectual, who is willing to leave London...when a man is tired of London, he is tired of life; for there is in London all that life can afford.'

Dr Johnson's former house, near Fleet Street, is now a museum about his life.

The Tate Gallery has a fine collection of ▲ paintings by London-born artist and poet William Blake. This work is called *Pity*.

SPECIAL EVENTS

Londoners' diaries need never be empty. Royal events, sporting fixtures and festivals of all sorts fill the city's year from beginning to end.

Winter mixture

Two contrasting events are held in London at the start of the year. On the last Sunday in January, a few people remember the execution of King Charles I in 1649 (see page 9). They dress in 17th-century clothes and lay a wreath where he died. In February there are joyful Chinese New Year celebrations. Thousands of people visit Chinatown to eat festive food and to watch firecrackers and dragon dances.

Spring events

The annual boat race between Oxford and Cambridge universities takes place on the Thames in March. The teams row over a four-mile stretch of the river. The London Marathon is run in April. Entrants pant their way from Greenwich to Westminster Bridge. In May plants of all sorts are displayed at the impressive Chelsea Flower Show, which is held in Christopher Wren's Royal Hospital.

▲ London Fashion Week is held twice a year, in spring and autumn. Shows feature the work of designers from all around the world.

▲ Many local children dress up and take part in the Notting Hill Carnival. Costumes and floats can take months to prepare.

The summer season

The Summer Exhibition is held at the Royal Academy from June to August. Anyone can submit paintings, but not all are chosen for display. Top players compete at the Wimbledon tennis championships in June and July. The Caribbean community runs the Notting Hill Carnival in August. For three days, costume parades and floats wind through the streets to the sound of reggae and other music.

ROYAL CEREMONIES

There are royal ceremonies throughout the year. The queen's official birthday in June is marked with an event called the Trooping of the Colour. This military drill is carried out on Horse Guards Parade, Whitehall, by soldiers of the **Household Cavalry**. The State Opening of Parliament (right) is in October or November. The queen rides by coach from Buckingham Palace to the Houses of Parliament. She enters the **House of Lords** and reads out the government's plans for the year.

▲ Representatives from Oslo, Norway, present their annual gift of a Christmas tree to officials of Westminster council.

In the autumn

The Promenade Concerts, known as the Proms, are classical music events held in the Royal Albert Hall from July to September. On the Last Night of the Proms, people wave flags and sing patriotic songs. Some people love the event, others think it is too rowdy. On Remembrance Sunday in November, the royal family, politicians and armed forces gather at the **Cenotaph** on Whitehall to remember Britain's war dead.

Christmas cheer

Lights and decorations brighten up London's streets during the Christmas season. The largest Christmas tree is always in Trafalgar Square. The city of Oslo in Norway has given the capital a giant tree every year since 1947. It is a sign of the country's thanks for its liberation by British troops during the **Second World War**. Trafalgar Square is traditionally the scene of London's noisiest New Year celebrations, though these are now strictly controlled by police.

Characters of all sorts have played a part in London's long and varied history. Here are just a few of the most famous names.

Richard Whittington

Dick Whittington is now known as a pantomime character. He leaves London with his cat, then hears bells chiming: 'Turn again Whittington, thrice Lord Mayor of London.' When he returns, the prediction comes true. In fact there was a real Richard (Dick) Whittington. He was a City merchant who served as mayor four times between 1397 and 1419. He also donated a great deal of money to charity.

▲ A portrait of Christopher Wren in front of his great masterpiece of architecture, St Paul's Cathedral.

Sir Christopher Wren

Christopher Wren was an astronomer who served as the president of the Royal Society (see page 21). His greatest claim to London fame is as an architect. After the 1666 Great Fire he built the new St Paul's Cathedral and at least 50 churches. Christopher Wren is buried in St Paul's. A Latin sentence on his tomb means: Reader, if you seek his monument, look around you.

Charles Dickens

The great novelist Charles Dickens arrived in London as a 10-year-old boy in 1823. He had to start work when he was 12 because his father was imprisoned for debt. Later, as a lawyer's clerk and political reporter, Dickens learned more about the harsh life of London's poor. He used his experiences and knowledge of the city in books such as *Oliver Twist*. One of his homes is now a museum.

▲ This painting of Charles Dickens at his writing desk hangs in London's Victoria and Albert Museum.

▲ Ellen Terry was a friend of the playwright George Bernard Shaw. They exchanged many letters, and Shaw wrote a play for her.

Ellen Terry

Ellen Terry was the greatest actress in late 19th-century London. Her on-stage partnership with Sir Henry Irving, the actor-manager of the Lyceum Theatre, lasted 24 years. Ellen Terry played many different roles, classical and modern, but her most well-known was as Ophelia in William Shakespeare's famous play *Hamlet*.

Ken Livingstone is famous for his ▲ left-wing politics – and for his love of amphibians, especially newts.

OCTAVIA HILL

In the 19th century, Octavia Hill helped London's poor by buying slums, renovating them, then renting them out at a fair price. This approach was so successful that it was copied in other cities such as Berlin in Germany. In 1895, Octavia Hill co-founded the **National Trust**. One of her own London homes now has a blue plaque on the wall (below). This is part of a scheme run by **English Heritage** to mark sites in the capital that are linked with famous people. The city has over 600 blue plaques.

Ken Livingstone

In 1981 Ken Livingstone became leader of the Greater London Council (GLC), which was the governing body of the capital. His policies, such as providing extra money for public transport, caused clashes with the national government. The government abolished the GLC in 1986 and Livingstone became **Labour** MP for Brent. In 2000, he won the election for mayor of London as an independent candidate (see page 42).

LONDON'S FUTURE

London will no doubt be an exciting place to live in the 21st century. But there are many challenges ahead. Poor areas need improving, and transport problems must be tackled.

◄ This photograph shows how the new Greater London Authority headquarters (the illuminated, circular structure on the right) may look.

The GLA

In 1998 Londoners voted to set up a new city government to be known as the Greater London Assembly (GLA). It was elected, together with a mayor (see page 41), on 4 May 2000. The architect Sir Norman Foster is building a stunning 'see-through' headquarters for the GLA on the south bank of the Thames.

Transport troubles

London's transport systems are under serious pressure and pollution caused by motor vehicles is increasing. The GLA has appointed a new Commissioner of Transport for London to improve all forms of public transport, particularly the Underground network. Robert Kiley, who began work in 2001, previously ran the New York City subway system.

Building work

Work is already under way on other important new buildings for the capital. Among them is the Spiral, an extension to the Victoria and Albert Museum. It was designed by architect Daniel Libeskind and its angular shape and ceramic-tile covering provide a striking contrast to the surrounding Victorian building.

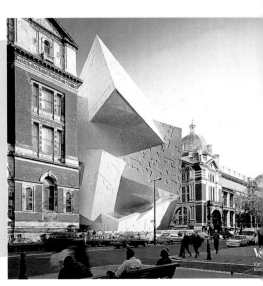

Some people think ► the design for the Victoria and Albert Museum Spiral is daring – others think it is disastrous. This image will help you to make up your mind.

Developing areas

The London Docklands Development Corporation has been rebuilding the docks area since trading ended there in 1981 (see page 24). Now London is expanding east as people and businesses move in. The South Bank is also developing fast. Its arts centre is to be rebuilt and the existing film complex made bigger. The GLA building, the new Tate Gallery and a new bridge (see box) have all added to growth south of the river.

The renovated Docklands warehouses ▲ are now large, luxury homes. Many belong to rich City business people.

Government changes

Important changes in the way Britain's government operates are being made. The role of the **House of Commons** altered in 1999 when Scotland got its own parliament and Wales its own **assembly**. The **House of Lords** changed, too, after reforms forced out all but 90 hereditary peers. These are lords who inherit rather than earn their title.

European role

The UK has belonged to the European Union since 1973, but it does not yet use the new European currency, the euro. Some people worry that cities such as Frankfurt will become more important financial centres than London. But at the moment the City's banks, exchanges and insurance firms are doing well and growing.

MILLENNIUM MAKEOVER

Several structures were built in London to mark the year 2000. The Millennium Dome (left) in Greenwich contained 14 zones, each dedicated to a different subject, such as work or play. Many people complained it was dull, but 6.5 million visited during the year. The Millennium Bridge across the Thames had to close because it swayed when people walked on it. Engineers are fixing the problem. Happily the London Eye ferris wheel on the south bank is a success.

TIMELINE

 This timeline shows some of the most important dates in London's history. All the events are mentioned earlier in this book.

1ST CENTURY AD

43
Romans invade England; Londinium is established

61
Queen Boudicca of the Iceni tribe burns down Londinium; Romans later defeat tribes and restore the city

5TH CENTURY

410
Roman rule of Britain ends; **Saxons** later settle west of Londinium and establish Lundenwic

9TH CENTURY

886
King **Alfred the Great** defeats the raiding **Vikings** and rebuilds the Roman city

11TH CENTURY

1016-1042
Danish Vikings rule part of England

1042
Edward the Confessor comes to the throne

1066
King Harold succeeds Edward
Harold defeated by invading **Norman** king William the Conqueror; William crowned

14TH CENTURY

1348-50
Black Death kills about half London's population

16TH CENTURY

1534
Church of England established

1536
London's monasteries shut by King Henry VIII

1558
Queen Elizabeth I comes to the throne

1599
First Globe Theatre completed

17TH CENTURY

1605
Gunpowder Plot against King James I fails

1642
English **Civil War** breaks out

1649
King Charles I beheaded

1649-1660
Period of **the Commonwealth**

1665
Great Plague hits London

1666
Great Fire destroys much of **the City**, including Old St Paul's Cathedral

1675-1711
Christopher Wren builds the new St Paul's

18TH CENTURY

1702

Fleet Street becomes centre of London newspaper industry

1705

Buckingham Palace completed

1759

British Museum opens

1798

Rules restaurant opens

19TH CENTURY

1801

London's population reaches about one million

1805

British navy led by Admiral Nelson defeats French at Battle of Trafalgar

1820

The Regent's Canal completed

1826

University College founded

1829

Metropolitan Police founded

1834

Palace of Westminster burns down

1837

Queen Victoria comes to the throne

1839

City of London Police established

1845

Potato famine in Ireland drives many Irish people to London

1863

London's first Underground line opens

1880

New law makes school attendance compulsory for children up to age of 11

1890

The Housing of the Working Classes Act becomes law

20TH CENTURY

1901

Death of Queen Victoria

1914-18

First World War

1918

Suffragettes win vote for women over 30

1939-45

Second World War; 30,000 Londoners die

1947

Many Indians arrive in Britain from India

1950s

Many people come to London from Caribbean

1953

Queen Elizabeth II crowned in Westminster Abbey

1960s

Many Indians arrive in Britain from Uganda and Kenya

1967-81

London's docks gradually close

1976

National Theatre opens

1981

Rebuilding of Docklands area begins

1982

Barbican Centre opens in City

1986

M25 road around London opens

1990

Poll Tax riot takes place in West End

1993

Black teenager Stephen Lawrence murdered

1997

New Globe Theatre opens

1999

Wales and Scotland have own *assemblies*
Millennium Dome opens

21ST CENTURY

2000

Mayor and Greater London Authority elected

GLOSSARY

Alfred the Great   A 9th-century ruler of Wessex, a Saxon kingdom in southern England. He pushed the Vikings back to areas north of London, then united the rest of England under his rule.

Anglican   A member of the Church of England or an associated church.

assembly   A group of people who meet to carry out official duties, such as government business.

asylum-seeker   A person who arrives from abroad seeking a safe place (asylum) in which to escape war or persecution.

basilica   A large building in which Roman officials carried out their public duties.

Black Death   A type of plague that spread from China to Europe. It was called the Black Death because it caused black marks on the skin.

Blitz, the   The 1940-41 period of heavy German air raids on London and other British cities during the Second World War.

British Empire   Britain and the many lands around the world that it once ruled. The empire began to grow in the early 17th century, and by 1918 covered more than a quarter of the globe. It declined from the mid-20th century, as more and more nations within it became independent.

British Summer Time   The time used in Britain from March to October. It is one hour ahead of Greenwich Mean Time.

Cenotaph   The monument to Britain's war dead that stands in Whitehall. It was completed in 1920. The word 'cenotaph' is Greek for 'empty tomb'.

Channel Tunnel   The rail tunnel underneath the English Channel between Britain and France. It opened in 1994.

City, the   The oldest part of London, which covers about one square mile (2.6 sq km) in the east. The City is a financial centre of world importance.

civil war   A war between different groups within a single country rather than between different countries.

Commonwealth, the   Britain between 1649 and 1660, when there was no king or queen.

digital   Broadcast in a way that provides better-quality pictures than usual.

East End   The area of Inner London that stretches east from the City. For many years the whole East End was poor, but redevelopment, for example in Docklands, has created some rich districts.

English Heritage   An organization set up by the government in 1983 to look after many of England's ancient monuments.

ethnic minority   A group of people belonging to a different race from most of the population.

FA Cup   A knock-out football competition set up by the Football Association (FA) in 1871.

First World War   A major war that lasted from 1914 to 1918 and involved many countries. Eventually Germany and Austria-Hungary were defeated by Britain, France, Russia and the USA.

forum   An open space where meetings and markets were held in Roman cities. London's forum was four times larger than Trafalgar Square.

Georgian   Of or relating to the period when four kings called George ruled Britain, one after the other. The period ran from 1714 to 1830.

Greenwich Mean Time   The time in Greenwich, England, which stands on the zero line of longitude. It is used as a base for calculating the time in the rest of the world.

Gunpowder Plot   The plot to blow up King James I and the Houses of Parliament in 1605. The plotters were Roman Catholics angry that the king had not made religious reforms. Their plan was discovered and most of them were hanged.

hectare An area the same size as 10,000 square metres.

House of Commons The chamber of the Houses of Parliament that is made up of elected MPs (Members of Parliament).

House of Lords The chamber of the Houses of Parliament that is made up of lords and ladies.

Household Cavalry The mounted (horse-riding) regiment that acts as the bodyguard of the king or queen.

Huguenots French Protestants, most of whom believed in the ideas of the Swiss religious leader John Calvin.

Industrial Revolution The changeover from a mostly agricultural to a mostly industrial economy. In Britain, this was between the mid-18th and mid-19th century.

Inn of Court A professional institution to which barristers belong. There are four – Lincoln's Inn, Gray's Inn, Inner Temple and Middle Temple. The Inns contain barristers' offices, called chambers.

IRA The Irish Republican Army, an organization that wants to unite Ireland by ending British rule in Northern Ireland. It has used bombs and other terrorist tactics to try to achieve its aims.

Labour Belonging to the Labour Party, one of the two main parties in British politics. It was originally a left-wing, socialist organization, but in recent years has become more moderate.

National Trust An organization that preserves buildings of historic importance in England, Wales and Northern Ireland.

Nazi Of or relating to the rule of Germany by the National Socialist German Workers' Party (the Nazi Party), led by Adolf Hitler. The Nazis were in power from 1933 to 1945 and persecuted the Jews and others.

New Towns Towns set up in Britain after the Second World War because there were not enough homes in the big cities. New Towns around London include Basildon, Harlow and Stevenage.

Norman Of or relating to the people of Normandy in northern France, who conquered England in 1066.

orthodox Keeping to strict rules and standards, for example religious ones.

pogrom An organized, violent attack, especially against Jews.

poll tax A tax on a person instead of on the person's income, wealth or property.

Puritan A strict Protestant, often a follower of John Calvin (see Huguenot). Puritans worship God in simple ceremonies and usually wear plain, dark clothes.

Rosetta Stone A black stone discovered in Rosetta, Egypt, in 1799. Egyptian and Greek writing on the stone helped experts to learn to read Egyptian hieroglyphics.

Royal Shakespeare Company (RSC) A company of actors that mainly stage William Shakespeare's plays. Plays appear first in Stratford-on-Avon (Shakespeare's birthplace) then go to the Barbican Centre in London.

Saxon A member of a Germanic people that invaded England during the 5th and 6th centuries AD.

Second World War A major war that lasted from 1939 to 1945 and involved many countries. Eventually Germany, Italy and Japan were defeated by Britain, France, the USSR and the USA.

Square Mile The City, which covers about one square mile (2.6 sq km).

Stuart Of or relating to the royal dynasty that ruled Britain from 1603 to 1714.

suburb A district on the edge of a city, not in the centre.

suffragette A woman who campaigned for voting rights (suffrage) for women.

Tudor Of or relating to the royal dynasty that ruled England from 1485 to 1603.

Viking A sea warrior from Denmark, Norway, or Sweden. Vikings invaded and settled in many countries from the 8th to the 11th century AD.

West End The wealthy area west of the City. Its first districts were Soho and Mayfair. The West End has since spread and contains many famous shops and theatres.

INDEX

Albert Memorial 6, 7, 15
Alfred the Great 8, 44, 46

Bank of England 4, 7, 25
Barbican Centre 7, 19, 34, 35, 45
Battersea Park 17
Bevis Marks Synagogue 23
Black Death 8, 44, 46
Blake, William 37
Blitz, the 11, 14, 46
Boudicca, Queen 8, 17, 44
Brick Lane 12, 13, 23
British Empire 10, 24, 46
British Museum 7, 36, 45
Brixton 13
Buckingham Palace 4, 7, 15, 39, 45

Canary Wharf 15
Cenotaph, the 7, 39, 46
Central London Mosque 6, 7, 23
Channel Tunnel 28, 46
Charles I, King 9, 38, 44
Chinatown 33, 38
Churchill, Winston 21
City, the 4, 5, 6, 7, 9, 16, 18, 23, 24, 25, 27, 28, 30, 31, 34, 43, 44, 46
civil war 9, 44, 46
Commonwealth, the 9, 44, 46
Covent Garden 7, 31
Cromwell, Oliver 9, 34
Crown Jewels 14
Crystal Palace 10
Cumberland Terrace 18
Cutty Sark 37

Dickens, Charles 22, 32, 40
Docklands 11, 15, 19, 25, 28, 31, 33, 43, 45
Docklands Light Railway 29
docks 11, 24, 45

East End 10, 13, 27, 46
Edward the Confessor 8, 14, 22, 44
Elizabeth I, Queen 9, 44
Elizabeth II, Queen 11, 39, 45

ethnic minorities 12, 13, 26, 46

Fawkes, Guy 9
First World War 10, 45, 46
Fleet Street 7, 19, 25, 33, 45

George I, King 10
George III, King 15
Georgians 10, 18, 26
Globe Theatre 7, 34, 44, 45
Golders Green 23
Greater London Assembly 5, 42, 43, 45
Great Exhibition 10
Great Fire of London 9, 14, 15, 18, 19, 40, 44
Great Plague 9, 44
Greenwich 37, 43
Gunpowder Plot 9, 44, 46

Hampstead Heath 17
Hampton Court 16, 17
Harold, King 8, 44
Henry VIII, King 4, 9, 14, 16, 22
Hill, Octavia 41
House of Commons 5, 43, 47
House of Lords 5, 39, 43, 47
Houses of Parliament 5, 7, 9, 14, 39
Huguenots 13, 23, 47
Hyde Park 6, 7, 16

Industrial Revolution 29, 47
Inns of Court 27, 47
IRA 11, 27, 47

Jack the Ripper 27
James I, King 9, 44
Johnson, Dr Samuel 7, 37

Kensington Gardens 16

Leicester Square 35
Livingstone, Ken 41
Lloyd's of London 7, 25
Londinium 8, 44
London Bridge 7, 8, 14, 26, 27, 45

London Marathon 38

Madame Tussaud's 6, 7, 36
Mayfair 31
Millennium Dome 28, 43, 45
Museum of London 7, 36

Nash, John 16, 18
National Gallery 7, 37
National Maritime Museum 37
Natural History Museum 6, 7, 36
Nelson, Admiral Horatio 5, 15, 37, 45
Nelson's Column 5, 7, 15
New Towns 19, 47
Normans 8, 47
Northern Ireland 4, 5
Notting Hill Carnival 38

Old Bailey 7, 27
Old Royal Observatory 37
Oxford Street 7, 30

Palace of Westminster 5, 14, 45
Peabody, George 18
Peel, Robert 21
Pepys, Samuel 19
Piccadilly 7, 31
Piccadilly Circus 7, 15
Poll Tax 11, 45, 47

Regent's Canal 6, 29, 31
Regent's Park 6, 7, 16, 18, 23, 29
Richmond Park 16
River Thames 4, 5, 6, 7, 8, 11, 14, 17, 34, 37, 38, 42
Romans 8, 12, 24, 44
Royal Albert Hall 6, 7, 35, 39
Royal Botanic Gardens 17
Royal National Theatre 7, 34
Royal Shakespeare Company 34, 47
Royal Society 21, 40

St James's Palace 4, 7, 9
St James's Park 7

St Paul's Cathedral 4, 7, 9, 15, 22, 40, 44
Salvation Army 23
Samaritans 23
Saxons 8, 44, 47
Science Museum 6, 7, 36
Scotland 4, 43, 45
Second World War 11, 13, 19, 25, 39, 45, 47
Senate House 21
Serpentine, the 6, 16
Shaftesbury Avenue 7, 34
Shaftesbury, Earl of 15
Shakespeare, William 4, 9, 34, 41
Soho 7, 33
Southwark Cathedral 22
Square Mile 4, 26, 47
Stock Exchange 4, 25
Stuarts 9, 47
suffragettes 10, 45, 47
Swaminarayan Temple 23

Tate Gallery 7, 37
Terry, Ellen 41
tourism 11, 24, 25
Tower Bridge 4, 7
Tower of London 7, 8, 14
Trafalgar Square 5, 7, 15, 37, 39
Tudors 9, 26, 47
Turner, Joseph 37

Victoria and Albert Museum 6, 7, 36, 40, 42
Victoria, Queen 10, 15, 45
Vikings 8, 44, 47

Wales 4, 43, 45
Wembley Stadium 35
West End 10, 16, 18, 30, 34, 4
Westminster Abbey 7, 8, 11, 22
Westminster Cathedral 7, 22
Westminster Hall 14
Whittington, Richard 40
William I, the Conqueror 8, 14, 44
Wren, Sir Christopher 9, 15, 21, 38, 40, 44